He Was One of Us

He Was One of Us

Rien Poortvliet

Baker Books

A Division of Baker Book House Co
Grand Rapids, Michigan 49516

It wasn't my intention in this book to try to sketch how Mary, Peter, or Barabbas looked; and certainly not Jesus' face as it might have been.

But because the familiar Bible texts can sound much too familiar to us, while for others they are incomprehensible, I have tried to tell the story of Jesus by letting faces and hands do the talking. Because faces and hands speak their own language, they can express more clearly the fact that the people who lived when Jesus was on earth were completely normal folk. There was nothing of the saint about them. They weren't any different from us and we can immediately recognize their outward behavior. Each of us is Peter and Thomas and Judas, and the innkeeper who, sorry though he was, had no room.

If while looking at the pictures you are not able to discover what is going on, reach for your Bible. The story of Jesus is found in the Gospels of Matthew, Mark, Luke, and John.

I'm very happy that Hans Bouma has written texts for the various pictures.

He does what nobody does

What is it that is characteristic about Jesus? It is tempting to pin down his divinity. That way you can keep some distance. He's got to remain a bit of a stranger. The more divine, the less dangerous. All too human is risky business. And it makes sense, doesn't it? It's not for nothing is it, that Jesus is called "Son of God"?

Of course, but not ahead of time. He gets this title only later. He first has to become it. It isn't that easy. It's the man Jesus with whom the Gospels are so taken. On that basis he becomes head of humanity. He lives as one completely original, authentic, consistent. He does what nobody does. He is the Just One. He knows what love is. He shares himself until the very end. He is a heartwarming brother, an indefatigable friend. Jesus is the man in whom God so ardently hoped. He didn't simply come out of the blue. Jesus answered people's expectation. God recognizes himself in him; he can find himself totally in him. Jesus is a great relief for God. At long last a man who is in his image and likeness without fail. Finally someone who fully lives in the Spirit. Jesus is truly a man of God. Or should we say: a Son of the Father? He has a right to that title. Little by little he seems indeed to be the one. It can't be wrong. Whoever lived as he lived must be "Son of God." The Roman centurion was right when he confessed: "Truly this was the Son of God." But to be able to choose sides with him, we'll need to stand, like him, next to the cross where Jesus experiences his humanity to the utmost.

That cross immediately brings us up short as to what is impossible about Jesus' humanity. He doesn't save it. In this world, inhuman through and through, he had to run amuck. He is irritating; he calls forth resistance. He unmasks us. What remains of us overagainst him, the truly human one? We hopelessly own what we are. This Jesus accuses us. He is an upstart, a spell-breaker. Isn't he a traitor, a danger for society? Wouldn't it be better if he disappeared?

This book can be looked on as an act of homage to Jesus' humanity. But this does not mean that the man Jesus is pictured on every page. You'll get to see much more often the people around him. Ordinary folk who uniquely characterize Jesus in his humanity through their genuinely human reactions to all that Jesus does. Rien Poortvliet is fascinated by everything that Jesus sets in motion. Looking at the people in this book, you know who Jesus is.

What kind of real, human reactions do we meet in this book? Reactions of surprise, wonderment, delight, devotion. But in addition to that—and especially—alienation, bewilderment, mockery, rejection, aggressiveness, hate.

He was one of us. He is the only truly human one who has "survived." But he doesn't leave us out in the cold. He is so much one of us that he is one with us. As far as he is concerned, his humanity is our humanity. He is happy only when we have taken over his way of being, so that we too as "sons and daughters of God" finally will appear as the men and women we are called to be.

Hans Bouma

An ordinary girl
nothing striking about her
she'll be getting married
the mother of Jesus
she is ordinary
enough for that

Mary, his beloved
so strange, so distant

What should he do?
Isn't he too much

to remain hers
to marry her

share her secret
even this secret?

Here she comes
the woman of her dreams

So you see once again
how God does his work

the child leaps up
in her womb—

a born herald
what he will be

Suddenly a child
and what a child !

And then even more
heavy taxation
on their land in Bethlehem

Roman officials
map it out
and determine the assessment

they have to be there
that might make a difference

In no time Mary will be due
but they start on their way

two people
who get nothing
handed to them

Not seeing him
you bring what you can into the house
it's already crowded enough.

He's sorry...
if they had been a bit earlier...
perhaps elsewhere...

that's how it started:
faces ajar
doors quickly shut again

closed,
tightly shut hearts

so it is always
incovenient
a thousand excuses

that's how it will end

No room
      with people
your family
owes you it.

thank God
the animals
are there too

Jesus shall
never forget it

Not for them –
despised outcasts –
they didn't count

Not for them ?
For whom else ?

Peace on earth
justice for the oppressed

the Lord who seeks
what is lost

A man   a woman
a child
so human
so inescapable

Here God holds
open house

He lets
himself be known

they know enough
the proof of God's fidelity
lies in their hands

the day of their lives!
Face to face with the child!
It makes them young again

the one thing left to them
is to praise and glorify

A light for Israel
a sun that rises
over the peoples

the wise men follow a light
the sought and found
king of their dreams

Come on, forget it.
It's too good to be true

this is not the future

the child must die.

What just began
is right away crushed

No crown.

A sword hangs over
the child's head

Any child
could be Jesus

Herod
takes no chances

Bethlehem drowns
in the blood

Herod
can relax

Jesus is alive.
He died

the death of his little
brothers and sisters

Just wait!

looking
listening
playing
discovering
dreaming

being thirsty
coming home
telling stories

growing up
learning a craft
making plans ...
the way it goes

He enjoyed things
forgot everything
just asked and talked

completely in his element
a child in God's house

And his parents looked
and looked

What's got into him?
they don't know him

Mary calls him up short
he should know his place

He baptize Jesus?
that's going too far
things turned upside down

But it must be so
Jesus belongs there
body and soul

A matter of
righteousness

the righteousness
that John loves

which will finally
cost him his head!

Jesus' too

He goes apart, catches his breath, the time has almost come
All alone
just some animals
just his God

What is he setting in motion?

His enemy doesn't allow him rest, but tries to convert him
He doesn't hunger after power, honor, possessions

He is perishing from hunger after justice
he yearns for peace
his enemy knows what he is up to

You have your work
you're building toward something
there's a woman
and children

And then the voice
of that stranger
that look   that gesture...

What are you supposed to do?
You're defenseless!
He's the one!

the only thing to do is
to follow him
cost what it might

unheard of

bewildering   staggering   dangerous
liberating   healing   a revelation   the end

this changes everything!

He says what really matters; now you know
this is a man who fulfills the law, a just one

a Man of God!

He attracts it, he can't do anything against it
pain, sickness, death — he hates it
his God has something else in mind

Peter's mother-in-law knew it

Jesus can count on him
He's a likely chap

Does he believe it himself?
He doesn't know what he is saying

Jesus is different
He does what nobody does

He is the just one
Who can hold out with him?

the foxes have holes
the birds have nests

But he – a vagrant –!
He's impossible

they'll reduce him to size
he really fancies himself to be something

seething with rage
the demons sweep the waves up

it's like the flood
the chaos at the beginning.

the disciples   in panic
but Jesus   he sleeps

the sleep of the just
completely master of the situation

Of course it's great what he is doing
(they have the greatest admiration for him)
but he's really got to go —

before it starts to cost
                              even more —

A miracle
   that he walks again?

A wonder
   that his sins
   are forgiven?

Take a look
at where he feels at home
He's a fine one!

A friend
of tax collectors and sinners

they're on to that.

those are disciples
Try to swallow all of that!

they don't believe, do they,
all that talk about the doctor
who needs to be with the sick?

They sure don't

Just walking somewhere—
what talk, what staring—
there's no end to it

Wherever he comes
they want things from him
hands everywhere

hands craving
after healing liberation
what warmth, what love!

How can he take it?
He is defenseless
a man of pain

familiar with sicknesses
he leaves a trail of joy
behind him

Yesterday she was
playing
laughing
singing

the one who is
the most saddened
is, of course, Jesus

A girl like that
shouldn't be dead

It can't be true
She's sleeping

He'll teach his enemy that
he should leave children well enough alone

He calls her name   as if it were possible
he takes her hand

                        and it is —!

Do they know what awaits them?

They'll despair
be mocked hated threatened persecuted

Their quiet life is a thing of the past

Either you belong to Jesus, or you don't

Now they have him
he can't escape now

the Sabbath-violator
the destroyer of the law

If they didn't realize it before,
look, he's at it again

What is he saying?
Mercy!
He, _Lord_ of the Sabbath?

That finishes him!

He doesn't want to
upset anyone
but his family is waiting
for him, for a long time now

Make sure that
he knows that

He really knows how to upset people

He always was a bit strange
but this takes the cake

listen to him —
the note that he strikes with them
guaranteed to irritate people
Where does he get the right?

A touch of modesty would help him
After all, who does he think he is?
the carpenter's son

Just send them home.

Without eating?

They still don't know him

How could he —
their friend   their brother
their light   their bread

He loves them so!

But five loaves
and two fishes?

Enough
for one who loves

But look! Just try it!
whoever shares,
multiplies

A blessing rests on it

Having gone through so much with him, they should have known better
But no one recognizes him   A ghost!   they scream
Jesus trembles, whatever he does, he is, and remains for them

a stranger —

That woman is beginning to be a pain
Jesus ought to do something about her

Unperturbable he walks on _____

The woman wouldn't think of giving up
she throws herself at his feet

But Jesus is unyielding
Bread is for the children

But the crumbs, she asks,
"Aren't they for the dogs?"

At this Jesus will not be outdone
that is what he calls faith

The disciples could use some of that...

whatever he does
they will not believe

the air is red   it teems with signs :

the lame walk   the dead live
the poor receive the gospel

healing and reconciliation
are not from out of the blue

They see it with their own eyes.
How are they supposed to see it ?

Never!
"What is Jesus thinking?"

He, Peter
has something else in mind

The same Peter
who just a little while ago
delighted Jesus
with his confession?
The same Peter
a satan

Gradually he changes before their very eyes
who is he, is he still one of them?

For a while they will see him as he is:

a man after God's own heart
the high point of God's joy
true son of his father

their eyes will not be able to bear it!

A child
listens a while
is expectant

thinks little of itself
finds it easy to kneel

plays a bit
sings

A child
laughs at itself

The disciples
are caught off base

Would that child —

but the child knows nothing

they go along reluctantly
Just a moment ago they were having such fun playing

At first they find Jesus strange
and why are those big men looking so angry?

But Jesus laughs
  makes a joke
  and how he can tell stories

It's as if they knew him for a real long time
A shame, that he has to leave so quickly

they follow him with their eyes
they still feel his hand on their heads

It's in John's name
you understand

You mustn't take it amiss

Of course,
there's no doubt possible

But you are the one,
    aren't you?

you'll be happy to see
that her two sons
will soon get a place of honor

they've earned it

She can ask, at least
she is, after all, their mother

Look, Mary
and Martha running

as if Jesus wasn't there on a visit

that's him.
    Can't he be himself
    the guest who is the host?

Isn't he the one who serves——?

Actually, no one is really happy with him
People grasp at a hope — ah, a little uprising

But that Jesus — a shabby king —

only the children,
they mean it

what's gotten into him?

She means well
  of course, this is his chance

and Mary, his mother
waited so long

What is he upset about?
He doesn't let himself be ordered about

certainly not by his mother

Got to see him
no matter what!

He makes himself
completely ridiculous

doesn't believe his ears
he runs home

open arms   another person
open heart   begins to live

the night is the safest
he might be seen

A real conversation would be premature
Nicodemus doesn't give himself away
He hides and defends himself

Slowly it becomes light
He hurries
less certain than when he came

Jesus' words
won't leave him alone
    seed of rebirth?

He'll find out!

He is different – what does he want?
She doesn't like that type

She doesn't let herself be known
Mocking, she stares at him
Discussion? Fine, she goes along

She becomes more and more unsure
he seems to know her –

Who is he?
just as he knows her

Failed again!
Will they ever trip him up?

"To Caesar what belongs to Caesar
To God what belongs to God"

Of course, to each his own
and God is the Lord

they won't be second best in that
ashamed they slink away

She gives it
with all her heart
it isn't much,
it weighs a lot for God
She gives herself

Like booty
they drag her along
triumphant

Caught in the act
she should be stoned —
or does he think not ?

Defiantly they look at him.
Soured women
stand there, chuckling

How he sets them back on their heels
the hypocrites — !

Of course, he's faithful
to the law of Moses
what do they think ?

But just for that reason

just let them throw
the first stone

if they dare !

She doesn't know why
but it has to be...
there is still time —

Jesus understands

He needed this —
it will be cold
and quiet enough

the disciples confront a riddle
Judas
        knows what he is up to

He pays close attention
he likes a lot of things about
Jesus, but this is too crazy ! !

He would never
forgive himself

but can Jesus ?
It's everything that he asks—

to be the least

His decision is set
he can no longer turn back

even if he wanted to

he, Peter
deny Jesus—?

then surely Jesus doesn't know him yet
he should know by now

Oh, well, he'll find out
the kind of man he has
in him—

At the critical moment
he meets his hour
alone
that is clear
even his best friends
are no longer up to it

even Peter
he can't count on

all alone
the worst is still to come

Why a kiss, now?
More deadly than outright
hostility is pretended friendship —
friendship which once was genuine

They should have realized that
   he, Peter
      was still there

Like a fury he lets loose,
slashing away

something touching about it
but also merely ridiculous
merely irritating

for the umpteenth time
a slap in the face
from his master

Will it never sink in
who Jesus is?

This is their day
they have waited for this
He is theirs—
they'll never let him loose again
Now, what does he have to say—?

Whatever he says
it will ruin him

It's true too
in a certain sense
and if they can help
Caiaphas with that
it's for a good purpose
they'll say
and moreover
it pays well

As if he couldn't give out a cheer
Finally — the case is coming to a close !

but he contains himself

faith

friend
brother
hope
salvation
resurrection
life

but he must die !

Confessed him as no other
promised him ardent fidelity
and he meant it

that's how he is —

if worst comes to worst
give the impression he had nothing
to do with him — doesn't know the man

while he loves him so much — !

It's their problem
they have Jesus
and that's what it was all about

Judas must be able to see
what will come of it
he knew what he was doing
didn't he?
he knew

He sits there
those accursed Jews too

OK, they'll get their way
Jesus may be innocent
his rest is also worth something to him

If only his wife had not
pestered him with that dream

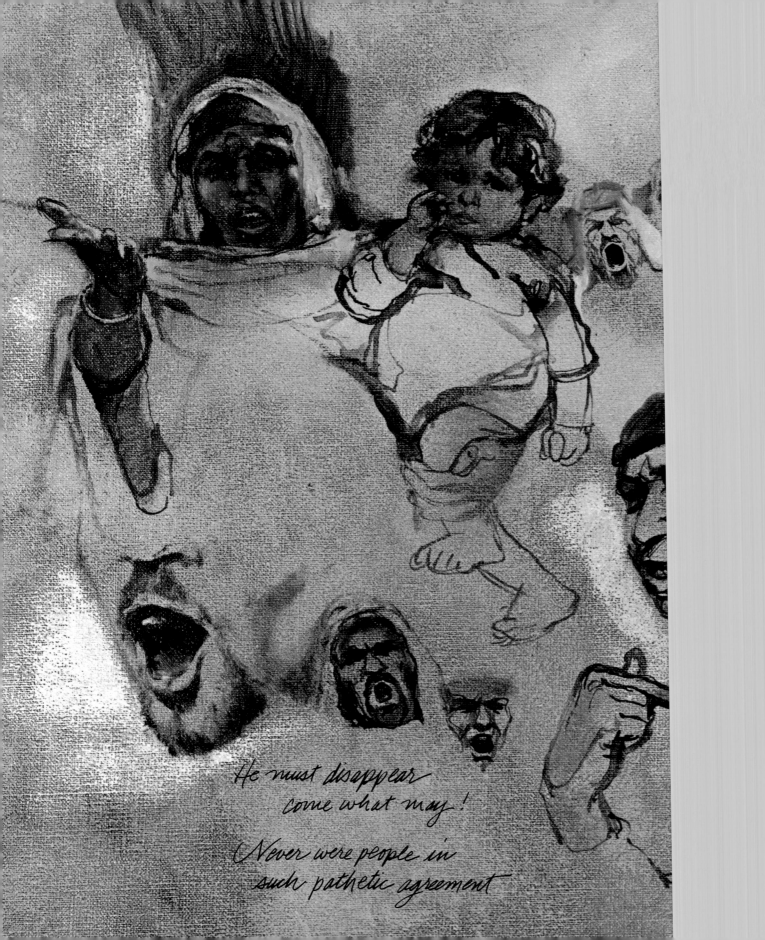

He must disappear
come what may!

Never were people in
such pathetic agreement

There isn't a mouth
which doesn't scream "Away with him!"
oh yes, that child there

A fine king
   to have sport with

he's getting what is coming
                to him
it won't be their fault

as though he was made of stone

They'll have their way with him
he has only himself to blame

they have their fill
boys will be boys

Now why him, a mere passerby?
    It will come out bad for him —
    he'd better get a move on.
He sees that he'd better obey
reluctantly he takes the cross on himself

It'll leave its mark on him
gradually he'll become a follower of Jesus

He will have to believe it now

expert
    hard as nails
    with great abandon

they pin him fast
    to his kingship

It's not just a matter of hanging
this is tough work!

But they do their work gladly
this character especially
gives them real satisfaction

But their centurion
could have been a bit more enthusiastic

What a day!
First that joke
that they played

and now he wins
his clothing as well

he won't
easily forget
that Jesus.

There you have him now
the Son of God

Now his God
nicely deserts him

He deserved it

Why didn't he just
act ordinary?

Or, is he the one
wonders one of them

To the very end
he remains reachable

a friend   a brother
a rescuer in need

But however he himself
searches and cries

no one can be found
no one
no human
no God

Mortal anguish he endures
all the mortal anguish
of all men and women

what he has seen
no one has seen
no one shall see again

He's finished!

He must be taken away

never again that voice
never again that look

they will have to go on
without him
the only thing
left for them

is to bury him

the final honor

Boring, this stupid tomb
couldn't Pilate have thought up something
a bit more enjoyable?

And if those disciples want to try something
just let them

...hey've just
...hrough!

...'d only keep
... mouths shut
...oles
...tolen him
...t's that
...y want
...re money?

She lives in another world
DEAD IS DEAD
everything ends.

the way he called her by name
It's Jesus
he's alive!

She's afire   the flames burst
with joy!   out of her

She starts living, at last

Who had counted on something like this ?
they had already resigned themselves to it

e – but
d to check
and that side.

hearts open up

If you don't believe me
then believe your eyes

but blessed is the one who
simply believes me — on my word

He wants to hear
it again and again

after everything
that has happened

he has good
reason for that

Now it all depends on them
Jesus entrusts everything to them

Will they continue his work?
Will they live in his spirit?

That spirit will be with them

List of Illustrations

...uke 1:26
...19
...Luke 1:39
...to Bethlehem   Luke 2
...Luke 2:7
...e inn   Luke 2
...ke 2:8
...Luke 2:16
...Luke 2:25–39
...he East   Matthew 2:1
...t   Matthew 2:13
...e innocents   Matthew 2:16
...Luke 2:40
...sus in the temple   Luke 2:41
...ohn   Matthew 3:13
...Matthew 4:1
...iples   Matthew 4:18
...e Mount   Matthew 5
...aw   Matthew 8:14
...Matthew 8:18
...Matthew 8:23
...ealed   Matthew 8:28
...d   Matthew 9:1
...e   Matthew 9:9
...vas sick for twelve years
...airus   Matthew 9:25
...e apostles   Matthew 10:1
...the Sabbath   Matthew 12:1
...he brothers of Jesus

...e town   Matthew 13:53
...nutiplication   Matthew 14:13
Jesus walking on the water   Matthew 14:22
The Canaanite woman   Matthew 15:21
Asking for a sign   Matthew 16:1
Peter is rebuked   Matthew 16:21
The transfiguration on the mountain   Matthew 17
The greatest in the kingdom   Matthew 18:1
Jesus and the children   Matthew 19:13
John the Baptist's question   Matthew 11:2
The rich man   Matthew 19:16

The mother of James and John   Matthew 20:20
Mary and Martha   Luke 10:38
The entry into Jerusalem   Matthew 21:1
The cleansing of the temple   Matthew 21:12
The marriage feast in Cana   John 2
Zacchaeus   Luke 19
Nicodemus   John 3
The Samaritan woman   John 4
Caesar's rights   Matthew 22:21
The widow's mite   Luke 21
The woman taken in adultery   John 8
The anointing   John 12
The washing of the feet   John 13
The betrayal foretold   Matthew 26:20
The denial foretold   Matthew 26:31
Gethsemane   Matthew 26:36
The Judas kiss   Matthew 26:49
Peter during the capture of Jesus   Matthew 26:51
Before the Sanhedrin   Matthew 26:57
False witnesses   Matthew 26:61
Caiaphas   Matthew 26:65
The judgment   Matthew 26:66
Peter's denial   Matthew 26:69
Judas   Matthew 27:3
Before Pilate   Matthew 27:11
"May his blood be upon us"   Matthew 27:25
The mocking   Matthew 27:27
The mocking   Matthew 27:27
Simon of Cyrene   Matthew 27:32
The crucifixion   Matthew 27:33, etc.
The crucifixion   Matthew 27:33, etc.
The crucifixion   Matthew 27:33, etc.
The murderers at the cross   Luke 23:39
"Eloi, Eloi . . ."   Mark 15:34
The darkness   Luke 23:44
After the crucifixion   John 29:38
The soldiers at the tomb   Matthew 27:62; 28:11
Easter, Mary of Magdala   John 20:11
The appearance to the disciples   John 20:19
Thomas and Peter   John 20:21
The ascension   Luke 24:51

anchor...

Little Portion
Treasures
1061 Market St.
Wheeling, WV
(304) 233-5782